FAMILY COOKBOOK

by Verner Center for Early Learning

For general information about other products and services, please visit our website, www.rainbowinmytummy.org, or contact us at:

Rainbow In My Tummy®

Verner Center for Early Learning
2586 Riceville Road
Asheville, NC 28805
Phone: 828-298-0808
Fax: 828-298-0707
info@rainbowinmytummy.org

*This cookbook is dedicated to the families,
caregivers and community advocates who work hard
to help our children grow up to be strong and healthy
leaders of tomorrow.*

Table of Contents

Acknowledgements

This Rainbow In My Tummy® family cookbook would not be possible without the financial support of the **Kate B. Reynolds Charitable Trust**. Their commitment has enabled us to extend our impact beyond the walls of early care and education centers and into the homes of young children by converting our most popular recipes into family sized portions.

Thank you also to the early care and education providers in western North Carolina that were early adopters of the Rainbow In My Tummy® program. They are the ones living out our mission: to improve the quality of food served to young children and cultivate a food culture that establishes a foundation for lifelong health.

There are also Verner staff members who have contributed in significant ways to the creation and expansion of the Rainbow In My Tummy® program. They include:

Susan Patrice, former Kitchen Manager, whose passion for cooking and desire to serve children a variety of colorful nutrient-rich foods is the reason why Rainbow In My Tummy® exists today. Susan, along with **Leslie Blaylock**, Director of Early Head Start, created the Rainbow In My Tummy® program and ensured that it received "two thumbs up" from young children and their families.

Genie Gunn, Food and Nutrition Manager, continues to model best practices in early care foodservice and sets a shining example for other centers to follow. Expect to see some of her recipes in our second edition!

Bronwen McCormick, Rainbow In My Tummy® Director, and **Kelly Brandon**, Director of Resource Development, have formalized and grown the program into a multi-state initiative. Their tireless commitment to Rainbow In My Tummy® has resulted in the program being used in early care and education centers in eight states and being recognized as a best practice by a variety of organizations.

Special acknowledgement goes to the Senior Nutrition majors at East Tennessee State University and Assistant Professor **Michelle Johnson MS, RD, LDN**, who converted all of the recipes in this book so they could be made at home, to **Kirsten Quatela of KQ Concepts Photography** and **Susan Patrice** who took the majority of the photos in this book, and to **Ginger Graziano**, cookbook graphic designer extraordinaire!

Finally, our deepest appreciation goes to **Jacque Penick**, Verner's Executive Director, **The Verner Board of Directors**, **The Community Foundation of WNC**, **United Way of Asheville and Buncombe County**, **The Community Benefit Program at Mission Hospital**, **Hugh and Danny Verner**, and **Rob Pew and Susan Taylor** for their ongoing commitment to Rainbow In My Tummy®. With their support and encouragement, Rainbow In My Tummy® has improved the quality of food served to thousands of children in early care settings across the United States.

WELCOME

As other early care and education centers began to adopt the Rainbow In My Tummy® program and introduce delicious new foods to the children in their care, one of the most frequently asked questions from parents has been: "How can I get these recipes? My child keeps asking me to make the food he has at school." Until now, all of our recipes have been written for food service production and designed to serve 25. We are excited to provide a tool and a resource to support healthy, delicious, and cost effective cooking and eating at home. We hope you enjoy these recipes and encourage the whole family to try new foods!

About Rainbow In My Tummy®

Rainbow In My Tummy® was developed by staff at Verner in 2008 to ensure that the young children they serve had access to a wide variety of healthy and delicious foods while in their care. Many children enrolled in early care centers eat two thirds of their daily calories while at a center. It's up to us to make those calories count!

Rainbow In My Tummy® has been either formally or informally recognized as a best practice by a variety of organizations including: the North Carolina Center for Health and Wellness, the Buncombe County Health Department, the North Carolina Institute of Medicine, and the Robert Wood Johnson Foundation and is a finalist for the 2015 Monroe Trout Premier Cares Award.

Rainbow In My Tummy® menus and recipes:

 Focus on the consumption of high-quality, nutritious, whole foods cooked from scratch.

 Eliminate ingredients such as trans fats, high fructose corn syrup, and artificial sweeteners and colors from the diet.

 Minimize amounts of sodium, sugar, and saturated fats.

 Increase intake of essential vitamins and minerals through a diet rich in a "rainbow of colors."

What is so great about Rainbow In My Tummy®?

Rainbow In My Tummy® is based on widely accepted and respected best practices and recommendations for food consumption by young children, including the following:

- USDA Dietary Guidelines for Americans (2010)
- USDA Child and Adult Care Food Program (CACFP)
- Head Start and Early Head Start
- Institute of Medicine (IOM) recommendations for Early Child Care (2011)
- IOM recommended revisions for CACFP (2011)
- Academy of Nutrition and Dietetics Benchmarks for Nutrition in Child Care (2011)
- American Academy of Pediatrics Recommendations for Prevention of Childhood Obesity (2007)
- Harvard School of Public Health
- Plus, all of the recipes have been KID-TESTED and KID-APPROVED!

×

What others are saying about Rainbow In My Tummy®

"We won a USDA Best Practice Award!" – Center Director

"Our food service costs actually went down!" – Kitchen Manager

"The Office of Head Start recently recognized our Rainbow In My Tummy® program as a strength." – Head Start Nutrition Director

"We've increased our use of fresh fruits and vegetables by 80%" – Center Director

"Children are less irritable in the afternoons." – Classroom Teacher

"My son opted for broccoli on a buffet bar!" – Parent

"We won a CACFP Healthy Menu Award!" – Center Manager

"Rainbow In My Tummy® has inspired us to be healthier at home." – Parent

About Verner

Verner Center for Early Learning is an Early Head Start provider and nonprofit early care and education program located in Asheville, North Carolina. Verner provides high quality, affordable care and education to roughly 200 children from birth to 5 years of age, Learn more at www.vernerearlylearning.org.

Verner
Center for Early Learning

Sample Breakfast Menus (Serve with milk or water)

Baked Apple French Toast
Blueberry Fruit Purée
(Blend 1 cup of frozen blueberries (thawed) + ¼ cup of water
to make puree. Strain if desired.)

Carrot Cake Oatmeal
Sliced Bananas

Protein Rich Fruity Granola
Pumpkin Pie Yogurt
Apple Slices

Apple Spice Muffins
Mango (fresh or frozen)

Very Berry Roll Up
Fresh pineapple

Sample Snack Menus (Serve with milk or water)

Sweet and Salty Cereal Mix
Sliced Pears

White Bean Dip
Whole Wheat Crackers

Wonderful Waffle Sandwich

Sweet Potato Hummus
Tortilla Triangles

Pizza Roll Ups

Sample Lunch or Dinner Menus (Serve with milk or water)

Red Lentil Stew with Coconut Curry
Brown Rice
Steamed Broccoli
Orange Slices

Turkey Meatballs
Marinara Sauce
Whole Wheat Pasta
Oven Roasted Brussels Sprouts

Spinach Lasagna
Spring Mix Salad
Sliced Fruit

Oven Baked Chicken Strips
Whole Wheat Bread Sticks
Edamame Succotash
Blueberries

Cuban Black Beans
Oven Roasted Sweet
  Potato Wedges
Toasted Tortilla Triangles
Sliced Cucumbers

Rainbow In My Tummy® Program Mission

The mission of Rainbow In My Tummy® is to cultivate a food culture surrounding young children that establishes a foundation for lifelong health. Through nutrition awareness and consumption of diverse, healthy, nutritious foods when tastes are first formed in young children, lifelong preferences for fresh, non-processed foods are promoted. The likelihood of obesity and obesity-related diseases now and in the future is reduced. What an incredible gift to give to our children!

Rainbow In My Tummy® strives to:

 Promote increased consumption of fresh and whole fruits and vegetables.

 Promote increased consumption of whole grains.

 Promote a decrease in the consumption of unhealthy fat.

 Promote a decrease in the consumption of sodium and added sugars.

 Promote a decrease in or elimination of the consumption of harmful ingredients.

 Provide opportunities for positive mealtime experiences and nutrition education enrichment that lead to a healthy food culture.

 Encourage positive, mealtime experiences for all ages of children.

 Emphasize the importance of water.

 Promote breastfeeding.

 Ensure that nutritional awareness and education occur in developmentally appropriate activities and learning opportunities.

 Promote modeling of healthy behavior.

Breakfast and Snack Recipes

 # Apple Spice Muffin

These moist muffins are full of chopped apples and a touch of cinnamon. This favorite has a tender texture that nicely complements the chewiness of the fruit.

INGREDIENTS:

1 cup whole wheat flour

1 cup all-purpose flour

1 teaspoon baking powder

1 teaspoon baking soda

1/4 teaspoon salt

2 teaspoons cinnamon

1/4 teaspoon nutmeg (optional)

1/2 cup unsalted butter, melted and cooled

1/3 cup brown sugar, packed

1/3 cup granulated sugar

1 large egg, beaten

1 cup low-fat buttermilk or non-fat yogurt

1 large apple, peeled, cored, and shredded

Makes: 12 muffins
Serving Size: 1 muffin

1. Preheat the oven to 400° F and line 12 muffin cups with paper muffin liners.

2. Combine the flours, baking powder, baking soda, salt, cinnamon, and nutmeg. Set aside. In a separate bowl, cream the butter and add the sugars. Beat until fluffy. Add the egg and mix well, scraping the sides and bottom of the bowl. Mix in the buttermilk gently. Stir in the dry ingredients, until moistened. Do not over mix. Fold in the shredded apple.

3. Fill each muffin cup 3/4 full. Bake for 18-20 minutes until golden in color and a toothpick inserted in the center comes out clean (these are moist muffins so the toothpick will always look a bit wet). Do not over bake. Cool the muffins for 5 minutes in the tin and then turn onto wire rack to cool. Muffins can be served warm, but are also delicious cool.

Baked Apple Cinnamon French Toast

This griddle-free version of a favorite breakfast treat can be prepared in advance and simply popped in the oven. The aroma of cinnamon and apples make it as enjoyable to smell as it is to eat.

INGREDIENTS:

2-3 apples, peeled, cored, and sliced

½ teaspoon cinnamon

⅛ teaspoon nutmeg

1 ½ tablespoon brown sugar

Dash of salt

4 tablespoons unsalted butter, melted

6-7 slices of whole wheat bread or whole wheat French bread

5 eggs

¼ cup half and half

½ teaspoon vanilla extract

¾ cup of milk, 1% or skim

Confectioner's sugar (optional)

Makes: 12 pieces
Serving Size: 1-2 pieces

1. Preheat oven to 350° F

2. In a large bowl, mix apples, cinnamon, nutmeg, salt, and brown sugar together. Add butter and stir to combine.

3. Generously coat a 9" x 11" pan with pan release spray or butter. Pour in apple mixture and spread evenly.

4. Cube bread and arrange evenly over the top of apple mixture.

5. In a large mixing bowl, whisk together eggs, half and half, milk, and vanilla. Pour mixture evenly over bread in pan. Cover and refrigerate for 6 hours or overnight.

6. Cover and bake for 25 minutes. Uncover and bake for 20-30 more minutes until golden brown and center has set.
   For an authentic French toast look, sprinkle a light layer of confectioner's sugar over French toast. Cut pan 3 X 4.

Blueberry Coconut Muffin

These muffins are well worth the time it takes to make them. The topping adds a crunchy texture to these moist and lightly sweetened muffins.

INGREDIENTS:

Topping:

¼ cup coconut

2 tablespoons brown sugar, unpacked

2 tablespoons all-purpose flour

1 tablespoon canola oil

Muffins:

¾ cup all-purpose flour

1 cup whole wheat flour

1 teaspoon baking powder

¼ teaspoon baking soda

⅛ teaspoon salt

½ teaspoon cinnamon

½ cup brown sugar, unpacked

1 tablespoon canola oil

1 large egg

1 large egg white

¾ cup non-fat buttermilk

2 tablespoons unsalted butter, melted

½ teaspoon coconut or vanilla extract

1 ½ cup fresh or frozen (not thawed) blueberries

Makes: 12 muffins
Serving Size: 1 muffin

1. Preheat oven to 400° F. Line 12 muffin cups with paper liners or coat with cooking spray.

2. To make topping, combine coconut, flour, and brown sugar in a small bowl. Drizzle with 1 tablespoon oil and stir to combine. Set aside.

3. To make muffins, whisk the flours, baking powder, baking soda, salt, and cinnamon in a medium bowl. Whisk the brown sugar, oil, egg, buttermilk, butter, and coconut (or vanilla) extract in a medium bowl until well combined. Make a well in the center of the dry ingredients and pour in the wet ingredients. Stir until just combined. Add blueberries and stir just to combine. Divide the batter among the prepared muffin cups. Sprinkle with the reserved coconut topping and gently press into the batter.

4. Bake for 20-25 minutes until the edges and tops are golden in color and a toothpick inserted in the center comes out clean. Do not over bake. Let cool in pan for 5-7 minutes before turning out onto a wire rack.

 # Cuban Black Bean Dip

Black beans provide support for our digestive tract health and are a wonderful protein-rich snack that give an extra boost of energy at the end of the day. This smooth and zesty dip is sure to engage little hands in dipping and food exploration.

INGREDIENTS:

2 teaspoons olive oil

2 ½ tablespoons onions, minced (about ¼ of a small onion)

3 cups (2 15-ounce cans) black beans, rinsed and drained (low sodium if available)

pinch garlic powder

2 tablespoons lime juice

1 tablespoon cilantro or parsley, chopped

1 tablespoon water

1 ½ teaspoons orange zest (optional)

pinch salt

1. In small skillet, heat oil and sauté onions until translucent. Set aside to cool.

2. Add all ingredients, including onions, to food processor. Pulse until desired consistency is reached.

Makes: about 2 cups
Serving Size : ¼ cup

Carrot Cake Oatmeal

This oatmeal is the perfect blend of crunchy, chewy, and sweet. Packed full of carrots and topped with coconut and pumpkin seeds, it is a hearty Vitamin A packed breakfast that will keep you satisfied all morning.

INGREDIENTS:

Oatmeal:

1 cup oats

1 cup milk, 1%, skim or soy

1 cup water

¾ cup carrots, shredded

½ cup pineapple, roughly chopped

Pinch of salt

½ teaspoon cinnamon

¼ teaspoon nutmeg (optional)

¾ tablespoon brown sugar, unpacked

½ tablespoon pure vanilla extract

Topping:

⅓ cup Greek style yogurt, non-fat

½ tablespoon maple syrup

2 tablespoons pumpkin seeds, roasted

2 tablespoons coconut, shredded

Makes: about 3 cups
Serving Size : ½ cup

1. Make oatmeal by combining oats, milk, water, carrots, pineapple, salt, cinnamon, and nutmeg in a saucepan. Turn heat to medium and stir occasionally until almost boiling. Cook until most of the liquid is absorbed, 6-10 minutes.

2. When oats are done, stir in brown sugar and vanilla.

3. Create topping by blending yogurt and maple syrup. To assemble, put ½ cup oatmeal in bowl, top with yogurt mixture, and then sprinkle pumpkin seeds and coconut on top.

Carrot Ginger Spread

Young children love the experience of dipping, and this brightly colored spread is both healthy and beautiful. This recipe has been modified for young taste buds. When serving adults, feel free to increase the curry and ginger to taste.

INGREDIENTS:

4 cups carrots, peeled and sliced

1" piece of fresh ginger, peeled and chopped

1 teaspoons mild curry powder

1 cup non-fat plain yogurt

½ cup olive oil

½ teaspoon salt

1 teaspoon apple cider vinegar

1 tablespoon brown sugar, unpacked (optional)

Makes: about 4 cups
Serving Size: ½ cup

1. Steam carrots and ginger over boiling water or in steamer until carrots are tender, about 10 minutes.

2. In a food processor or blender, purée carrots and ginger with remaining ingredients until smooth.

> IT IS EASY to incorporate fruits or vegetables into healthy dips and spreads. Orange vegetables such as sweet potatoes, pumpkin, butternut squash, and carrots are full of nutrients including Vitamin A, manganese, iron, fiber, and antioxidants (to name a few). They also have a slightly sweet taste which can satisfy a craving for something sweet.

Pizza Roll Up

This easy pizza-inspired roll up is a kid pleaser. The whole wheat tortilla helps add needed fiber without any fuss. Stuff with your favorite veggies for added color and flavor.

INGREDIENTS:

4 whole wheat tortillas, 8" or 10"

½ cup (4 ounces) marinara sauce

1 cup mozzarella part-skim cheese, shredded

¼ large onion, chopped and sautéed

½ yellow pepper, chopped and sautéed

¼ cup mushrooms, sliced and sautéed

(Feel free to use any combination of sautéed or roasted vegetables. They should total 1 cup for this recipe.)

Makes: 8 pieces
Serving Size: 1 piece

1. Preheat the oven to 350° F.

2. Lay tortillas on flat surface. Spread 2 tablespoons (1 ounce) marinara sauce. Sprinkle with ¼ cup cheese.

3. Combine sautéed vegetables and add ¼ cup to each tortilla.

4. Roll each tortilla into a log. Place on baking sheet with rolled end down (to hold it in place). Bake for 10 minutes. Let cool for 3 minutes and cut each roll up in half.

PURCHASE NOTE:

If you are using prepared marinara sauce, choose one that does not contain high fructose corn syrup and has less than 350mg sodium per ½ cup serving. (Less than 300mg sodium per ½ cup is even better!)

Protein Rich Fruity Granola

Full of whole grains, seeds, and dried fruit, granola is easy to prepare and when made from scratch, it is much lower in sugar and higher in protein. This recipe makes extra. Seal tightly for later use.

INGREDIENTS:

2 cups rolled oats

¾ cup sunflower or pumpkin seeds

1 teaspoon cinnamon

¼ teaspoon salt

¼ cup canola oil or a mild olive oil

2 tablespoons honey or brown rice syrup

1 tablespoon + 1 teaspoon brown sugar

½ teaspoon vanilla extract

¾ cup shredded coconut

¾ cup dried fruit*, chopped

*use at least two different kinds of fruit

Makes: about 6 cups
Serving Size: ½ cup

1. Preheat oven to 300° F. In large bowl, combine rolled oats, sunflower seeds, cinnamon, and salt

2. In medium bowl, combine oil, honey, brown sugar, and vanilla and whisk to combine. Pour liquid mixture over the oat mixture and stir until the oats and seeds are coated.

3. Spread evenly in a thin layer on a sheet pan. Leave an inch border between the granola and the edge of the sheet pan.

4. Cook for about 20-30 minutes, stirring every 5 minutes. Gently move granola from outer edges of pan to the center with a spatula. Add shredded coconut during the last 5 minutes of baking.

4. When granola is golden brown, remove from oven. Allow to cool for 10 minutes. Stir in dried fruit and allow to cool completely before transferring to a sealed storage container. Granola freezes very well.

GRANOLA PARFAITS are a fun and delicious way to make snack time a special occasion or to build a healthy dessert! Layer yogurt and granola in a parfait cup or small bowl by placing ¼ cup of granola in the bottom of the cup, top with ¼ cup plain or vanilla yogurt, add a layer of fruit, and then top with remaining granola.

# Pumpkin Muffin

Pumpkin makes this muffin fluffy and flavorful. The puréed pumpkin loads this muffin with vitamin A. Its orange coloring and festive flavoring will remind you of fall.

INGREDIENTS:

1 cup all-purpose flour

1 cup whole wheat flour

1 teaspoon baking soda

½ teaspoon salt

1 teaspoon cinnamon

¼ teaspoon ginger

¼ teaspoon cloves

¼ teaspoon nutmeg

¾ cup brown sugar, packed

3 tablespoons molasses

¼ tablespoon vegetable oil

2 large eggs

1 cup 100% pumpkin purée

1 teaspoon vanilla extract

¾ cup fat-free buttermilk

Makes: 12 muffins
Serving Size: 1

1. Preheat oven to 400° F and line 12 muffin cups with paper muffin liners.

2. In large bowl or mixer, combine flours, baking soda, salt, cinnamon, ginger, and nutmeg.

3. In separate bowl, whisk together sugar, molasses, oil, and eggs. Whisk in pumpkin and vanilla. Add to flour mixture, alternating with the buttermilk. Mix until all pumpkin mixture is well combined with flour mixture. Do not over mix.

4. Fill each muffin cup ¾ full. Bake for 20 minutes until golden in color and a toothpick inserted in the center comes out clean (these are moist muffins so the toothpick will always look a bit wet). Do not over bake. Cool the muffins for 5 minutes in the tin and then turn onto wire rack to cool. Muffins can be served warm, but are also delicious cool.

TIP:

No buttermilk? No problem! Just add a little lemon juice to regular milk (1 tablespoon per 1 cup of milk) and let it sit for 10 minutes.

Pumpkin Pie Yogurt

This creamy festive yogurt is like having a piece of pumpkin pie, but is better for you! Yogurt helps improve the absorption of Vitamin A, which is found in abundance in pumpkin. It is also great for growth, appetite, and eyesight!

INGREDIENTS:

2 ½ cups unsweetened non-fat yogurt

½ cup 100% pumpkin purée

¼ cup pure maple syrup

Cinnamon, pinch

Ginger, pinch

Cloves, pinch

PURCHASE NOTE:

Look for pure maple syrup or a table syrup that is high fructose and corn syrup-free and contains no artificial flavors or colors.

Makes: about 3 cups
Serving Size: ½ cup

1. In large bowl, mix all ingredients thoroughly. Cover and refrigerate until ready to serve.

> **NOTE:** The American Academy of Pediatrics recommends waiting until a child is at least one year old to serve honey, maple syrup or corn syrup (dark or light).

> Breakfast cereals can contain a lot of added sugar. When shopping for breakfast cereals, look for those that contain less than 6 grams of sugar per ounce (about 28.3 grams).

Scoop It Up Cheese Spread

Little ones love the interactive pleasure of dipping, and this reduced-fat adaptation of a classic Southern cheese spread makes scooping healthy and delicious.

INGREDIENTS:

3 ounces low-fat cream cheese

⅓ cup low-fat mayonnaise

½ teaspoon onion powder

⅛ teaspoon granulated garlic

2 tablespoons pimentos, drained, patted dry, finely chopped

¾ cup reduced-fat sharp cheddar cheese, shredded

½ cup reduced-fat Monterey jack cheese, shredded

Makes: about 1 ½ cups
Serving Size: 2 tablespoons

1. In mixer, blend cream cheese until smooth. Add mayonnaise, onion powder, and granulated garlic and mix until well combined.

2. Fold in pimentos and shredded cheeses. Refrigerate until ready to serve.

PURCHASE NOTE:

Look for mayonnaise that contains no high fructose corn syrup (HFCS) or corn syrup.

Sweet and Salty Cereal Mix

High fiber cereal takes on a new twist when mixed with sweet and chewy dried fruit and protein-rich seeds. This is a great way to use leftover cereal. Kids love it!

INGREDIENTS:

½ stick (2 ounces) unsalted butter, melted

1 ½ tablespoons brown sugar, unpacked

1 ½ tablespoons Worcestershire sauce

1 cup small pretzels

1 ½ cups Multi-Grain Cheerios or similar cereal

¾ cup Rice Chex

1 cup Wheat Chex

½ cup sunflower or pumpkin seeds

½ cup dried fruit, chopped

Makes: about 5 cups
Serving Size: ½ cup

1. In small bowl, mix butter, brown sugar, and Worcestershire sauce.

2. Heat oven to 250° F. Combine pretzels, cereals, and seeds in a large bowl and mix well. (Do not add dried fruit until after cooking.)

3. Pour butter mixture over cereal and stir to coat.

4. Pour mixture onto an ungreased baking tray and spread evenly. Bake for 1 hour, stirring every 15 minutes.

5. Remove from oven and mix in chopped dried fruit while cereal is still warm. Set aside to cool completely (approximately 30 minutes). Store extra mix in a sealed container.

Sweet Potato Hummus

This lovely orange-colored hummus is both sweet and savory. Sweet potatoes help support healthy eyes and immunity. Serve with sweet vegetables so children can scoop up these protein-rich beans.

INGREDIENTS:

1 pound sweet potatoes, peeled and cubed (about 2 cups)

1 ½ cup (1 15-oz can) cooked chickpeas, drained and rinsed

¼ cup lemon juice

¼ cup tahini paste

2 tablespoons olive oil

1 teaspoon cumin (optional)

½ teaspoon granulated garlic or one clove of fresh garlic, minced

¼ teaspoon salt

1 tablespoon brown sugar

1. Fill pot with about 2 inches of water. Bring water to a boil. Add cubed potatoes and cover. Reduce heat and steam for 10-12 minutes.

2. When potatoes are fork tender, drain, reserve the cooking liquid, and cool.

3. Add potatoes and all other ingredients to a food processor. Blend until smooth. Add reserved cooking liquid or warm water to adjust consistency. Refrigerate until ready to serve.

Makes: about 3 cups
Serving size: ¼- ½ cup

TAHINI PASTE is made from ground sesame seeds. It is a classic ingredient in Middle Eastern foods such as hummus. Tahini is a source of healthy fats such as omega-3 and omega-6. Look for it in the peanut butter or ethnic foods section of many grocery stores.

Very Berry Roll Up

Soft whole grain tortillas, creamy cheese, and tart strawberries are all rolled into one! Children will love seeing all of these ingredients spiraled together in this tasty snack. Use any favorite fruit or vegetable for seasonal variety.

INGREDIENTS:

2 whole wheat tortillas (8-10 inch)

½ cup reduced-fat cream cheese

½ cup strawberries, sliced

Makes: 10 pieces
Serving Size: 1 piece

1. Spread cream cheese on tortilla; sprinkle with the sliced strawberries and roll tightly.

2. Cut each roll into 5 equal pieces.

Encourage your child to try new foods by pointing out the sensory qualities of foods. Instead of saying, "You need to eat this food," try using statements like these: "This is a mango. It is sweet like a peach." Or, "These peppers are very crunchy!"

If strawberries are out of season, use ¼ cup of 100% fruit jam instead.

White Bean Dip

Little ones love the interactive pleasures of dipping and this mild bean dip is healthy and fun.

INGREDIENTS:

1 ½ cups (1 15-ounce can) great Northern beans, drained and rinsed

pinch of salt

1 tablespoon olive oil

¼ teaspoon lemon zest

1 teaspoon lemon juice

⅛ teaspoon fresh rosemary, chopped

1 clove fresh garlic, minced (or ⅛ teaspoon garlic powder)

Makes: about 1 ½ cups
Serving Size: 2 tablespoons

1. Blend all ingredients in food processor until smooth. If dip does not become creamy, add hot water one tablespoon at a time and blend until creamy.

2. Refrigerate until ready to serve.

> **AMERICANS LOVE SALT.** Unfortunately, this can lead to conditions such as high blood pressure and heart disease. A study from the Centers for Disease Control and Prevention (CDC) reports that many of the packaged foods marketed for children contain too much sodium. Not only does this put a child's long-term health at risk, but can cause them to develop a preference for salty foods early in life.

Whole Wheat Cinnamon Pita Triangles

You can make your own pita chips in a matter of minutes. Not only do they save you money, but they also cut fat and calories. Use whole wheat pita for extra fiber and a wonderful rich flavor and texture.

INGREDIENTS:

3 whole wheat pitas (6-7 inch in diameter)

1 tablespoon unsalted butter

2 teaspoons sugar

½ teaspoon cinnamon

Makes: 6 servings
Serving Size: 4 triangles

1. Preheat oven to 350° F. Coat a baking sheet with no-stick cooking spray or line with parchment paper.

2. Using kitchen shears or a sharp knife, cut around perimeter of each pita bread to yield thin rounds (6 slices) and stack the pita rounds. Using a large knife, cut them into 8 pieces (24 triangles).

3. Brush triangles with melted butter. In small bowl, combine sugar and cinnamon. Sprinkle cinnamon sugar evenly over buttered triangles.

4. Bake pita chips 7-10 minutes, until crisp. Watch closely at the end; crispy chips turn to burnt chips very quickly.

SAVORY PITA CRISPS

For a savory version, replace the butter, sugar, and cinnamon with:

1 ½ tablespoons olive oil

½ teaspoon cumin

¼ teaspoon garlic powder

¼ teaspoon kosher salt

Wonderful Waffle Sandwich

Kids love these! Whole wheat waffles are a wonderful sandwich surprise. Sunflower butter is a great-tasting alternative to peanut butter, with one third less saturated fat and a much higher iron and fiber content.

INGREDIENTS:

6 whole wheat waffles, frozen

6 tablespoons sunflower butter (or other nut butter)

3 tablespoons maple syrup

1 medium banana, sliced

Makes: 6 servings
Serving size: 2 triangles or ½ a sandwich

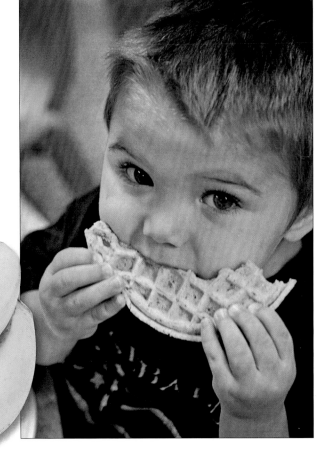

1. Preheat oven to 350° F. Spread 2 tablespoons nut butter on 3 of the frozen waffles. Drizzle 1 teaspoon maple syrup over nut butter and top with a layer of sliced bananas. Top with second frozen waffle and place on sheet pan.

2. Bake until warmed through. Cut each waffle sandwich into four triangles.

Vegetable Recipes

Black-Eyed Pea and Corn Salad

This delicious salad features black eyed peas, which get their name from their characteristic appearance. It is a fiber rich, high protein, colorful, and zesty snack that is so tasty you might forget the tortilla chips.

INGREDIENTS:

pinch of salt

2 cups fresh or frozen black-eyed peas

1 cup frozen corn

7 ounces tomatoes with mild green chilies (about half a 15 ounce can)

1 tablespoon onion, finely chopped

1 tablespoon cilantro, fresh, finely chopped

2 ½ tablespoons apple cider vinegar

¼ cup olive oil

¼ teaspoon sugar

pinch of granulated garlic

pinch of onion powder

salt and pepper to taste

1. Bring 2 ½ cups of water and a pinch of salt to a boil. Add black-eyed peas and cook for 30 minutes. Add corn and cook for an additional 2 minutes. Remove from heat, pour into colander, and rinse with cold water. Drain all water.

2. Transfer black-eyed pea and corn mixture into a large bowl and add remaining ingredients. Toss all together and let marinate for at least 2 hours or overnight before serving. Serve chilled with tortilla chips or multi-grain crackers.

Makes: about 3 cups   Serving Size : ½ cup

TOASTED TORTILLA Triangles are the perfect match for this salad and are super easy to make. Preheat the oven to 375°F. Brush 4 whole wheat tortillas with olive oil. Stack the tortillas and cut into 8 triangles. Arrange triangles in one layer on a baking sheet and bake for 7-9 minutes or until crispy.

Broccoli Slaw

Broccoli slaw is made from the tender hearts of fresh broccoli. Add a splash of carrots and red cabbage for color and flavor. It is a crispy, crunchy, alternative to traditional coleslaw.

INGREDIENTS:

12 ounces (about 3 cups) broccoli slaw mixture (shredded broccoli, carrots, and red cabbage)

¼ cup plain low-fat yogurt or reduced-fat sour cream

¼ cup reduced-fat mayonnaise

1 teaspoon brown sugar, unpacked

1 teaspoon vinegar or lemon juice

½ teaspoon salt

OPTIONAL ADDITIONS:

½ cup pineapple

½ cup chopped pears

1. Combine the shredded broccoli, cabbage, and carrots in a large bowl.

2. In small bowl, make the dressing by whisking together yogurt, mayonnaise, salt, brown sugar, vinegar or lemon juice, and salt.

3. Pour dressing over cabbage mixture and toss to coat. Cover and refrigerate until ready to serve.

> Explore food and where food comes from by visiting a farm or a farmer's market. Grow a garden. It doesn't have to be big—you can even grow one in a pot. Children who grow their own food are more likely to eat fruits and vegetables, show higher levels of knowledge about nutrition, and continue healthy eating habits throughout their lives.

Makes: about 3 cups
Serving Size: ½ cup

Carrot Salad

This tasty carrot salad with raisins and apples is beautiful and delicious enough to make a healthy eater out of all of us.

INGREDIENTS:

1 medium apple, peeled and small diced

2 teaspoons lemon juice, divided

3 cups carrots, coarsely shredded

½ cup raisins or currants

2 tablespoons plain non-fat yogurt

¼ cup low-fat mayonnaise

Salt to taste

Makes: about 3 cups
Serving Size: ½ cup

1. Toss apples with 1 teaspoon of lemon juice to keep them from browning. Combine carrots, raisins/currants, and apples in large bowl.

2. In separate bowl, combine yogurt, mayonnaise, salt, and remaining lemon juice (1 teaspoon) to make the dressing. Pour dressing over carrot mixture and mix lightly. Cover and refrigerate until ready to serve.

To keep portion sizes in check and encourage children to serve themselves the right amount of food for their bodies, use smaller "kid size" plates, bowls, and utensils.

Edamame Succotash

Replacing lima beans with edamame gives this traditional Southern dish an inspired update. Edamame have a buttery and nutty flavor with a wonderfully crisp texture. They are loaded with fiber and are a wonderful high-protein alternative to lima beans.

INGREDIENTS:

1 ½ cups shelled edamame (fresh or frozen)

1 ½ cups corn kernels (fresh or frozen)

2 tablespoons unsalted butter

1 teaspoon Spike seasoning (or season to taste with salt and pepper)

Makes: 3 cups
Serving Size: ½ cup

1. Mix edamame beans and corn together in large bowl. Steam for 5 minutes.

2. Remove from steamer and toss with butter and Spike.

EDAMAME in the pod makes a great snack or vegetable side. You can find them in the frozen food section of the grocery store. Empty an 8-10 ounce bag into a saucepan and add a half inch of water. Cover tightly and steam on high heat for 4-5 minutes. Drain excess water and lightly season with salt. The beans easily pop out of the pod and are a tasty and interactive snack!

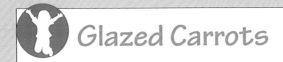

Glazed Carrots

These lightly glazed carrots, with a hint of cinnamon and butter, are great served warm as a side or as a sweet afternoon snack. When served as a snack, glazed carrots are delicious when paired with vanilla yogurt.

INGREDIENTS:

3 cups baby carrots or carrot coins

3 tablespoons unsalted butter

4 tablespoons water

4 tablespoons pure maple syrup (or brown sugar, unpacked)

2 tablespoons orange juice

½ teaspoon ground cinnamon

1 pinch ground allspice

1 pinch salt

Makes: about 3 cups
Serving Size: ½ cup

1. Place all ingredients in medium-sized heavy saucepan.

2. Bring to boil over medium high heat, stirring occasionally, until carrots are tender and sauce becomes a shiny glaze, about 10-15 minutes. Remove from heat and serve.

Maple and Cinnamon Roasted Beets

These maple caramelized beets are low in fat, but high in fiber and Vitamin C. Beets are great for cardiovascular health and help lower cholesterol levels in the body. They are even a fun food to eat. Kids love when they turn their tongues purple.

INGREDIENTS:

2 pounds fresh beets (without tops)

2 tablespoons unsalted butter, melted

2 ½ tablespoons pure maple syrup

½ lemon, zest and juice

1 tablespoon cinnamon

Makes: about 3 cups
Serving Size: ½ cup

1. Heat oven to 400° F. Thoroughly wash beets. Peel and cube. Place beets in roasting pan, cover, and cook for 30 minutes.

2. In bowl, mix butter, maple syrup, lemon juice, lemon zest, and cinnamon. Pour over beets, toss to coat, re-cover, and bake for another 30 minutes or until beets are tender.

NUTRITIONAL FACT: Juice contains about the same amount of sugar as soda. Even though juice has natural sugars versus the high fructose corn syrup found in many sugary beverages, it just about matches ounce for ounce the total amount of sugar. If you offer juice, make sure it is 100% pure fruit or vegetable juice and limit it to no more than 4-6 ounces per day. Even better, try serving water, low-fat, or skim milk instead.

Oven Roasted Brussels Sprouts

The Brussels sprout is a cultivar of wild cabbage grown for its edible buds. Not only are they high in fiber, but they also belong to the disease-fighting cabbage family and may actually help protect against some kinds of cancer.

INGREDIENTS:

1 pound fresh Brussels sprouts, trimmed, washed, and drained

2 tablespoons olive oil

1 teaspoon Spike seasoning (or season lightly with salt and pepper)

½ teaspoon garlic powder

Makes: 3 cups
Serving Size: ½ cup

1. Preheat oven to 350° F. Shred Brussels sprouts by slicing thinly or using a food processor (slicing blade).

2. In large pan, toss sprouts with olive oil, salt-free seasoning, and garlic. Spread evenly on baking sheet. Cook in oven, tossing occasionally, for 30-40 minutes or until slightly brown.

WE LOVE ROASTED VEGETABLES. Roasting brings out the natural sweet and nutty flavor of many vegetables. Follow these steps for a simple and delicious side dish.

Preheat oven to 400°F. Trim or cut vegetables into similar, consistent sizes. Add enough olive oil to coat and season with salt, pepper, and a pinch of garlic powder. (You can get creative with flavors and other spices as well.) For tender vegetables like asparagus or green beans, roast for 12-15 minutes. For root vegetables like sweet potatoes, beets, or turnips, roast for 35-45 minutes or until tender. Cooking times will vary depending on the size of the pieces. You can use this same method to make sweet potato or other vegetable "fries." Just cut them into sticks.

Oven Roasted Potato Wedges

Yukon Golds make for crispy and flavorful oven roasted potatoes and are a year-round hit. Cut them into wedges or fries and roast to a beautiful golden brown.

INGREDIENTS:

2 pounds Yukon gold (or russet) potatoes

2 tablespoons olive or canola oil

1 teaspoon Spike seasoning or lightly season with salt and pepper

½ teaspoon garlic powder

1 tablespoon Parmesan cheese, grated

2 teaspoons fresh chopped parsley

Makes: about 5 cups
Serving Size: ½ cup

1. Preheat oven to 450° F. Wash potatoes, drain, and pat dry. Do not peel. Cut each potato into six wedges or sticks (for fries). If not using immediately, cover with cold water to prevent browning/discoloration.

2. In bowl, toss potatoes with oil, seasoning, and Parmesan cheese. Line a sheet pan with parchment paper or spray with non-stick cooking spray. Distribute potatoes evenly; do not crowd.

3. Bake for 30-40 minutes. Turn potatoes over after 15 and 30 minutes for even cooking. Bake until golden and crisp. Garnish with chopped parsley.

Parmesan Roasted Cauliflower

Cauliflower is low in fat and high in fiber and Vitamin C. Roasting helps bring out its natural nutty flavor. Paired with a sharp cheese, like Parmesan, these golden brown roasted vegetables will become a mealtime favorite.

INGREDIENTS:

1 pound ready to use cauliflower florets or 1 head fresh cauliflower cut into florets

1 teaspoon granulated garlic

1 tablespoon lemon juice

1 tablespoon olive oil

Pinch of salt

2 tablespoons Parmesan cheese, grated

Makes: about 3 cups   Serving Size: ½ cup

1. In medium saucepan, lightly steam cauliflower florets for 2-3 minutes. Drain thoroughly and pat dry.

2. In large bowl, combine garlic, lemon juice, olive oil, and salt. Add cauliflower and toss to coat. Sprinkle with Parmesan and toss again.

3. Preheat oven to 400° F. Spread cauliflower in one even layer on greased baking sheet. Roast in oven, uncovered, for 15-20 minutes. Test with fork for desired doneness.

STEAMING VEGGIES

Steaming is a quick, healthy way to cook vegetables. Add about an inch of water to the bottom of a saucepan. (Add a steamer basket if you have one.) Place pot over high heat and bring to a boil. Add vegetables and cover with a tight lid. When the pot starts to steam, turn heat down to medium and cook for desired length of time. Check the vegetables after a few minutes. Tender veggies will take just a few minutes while denser vegetables will take longer.

Sautéed Kale with Caramelized Onions

Kale is one of the healthiest vegetables around. One way to be sure to enjoy the maximum nutrition and flavor from kale is to sauté it in olive oil. Slightly bitter kale is paired perfectly with sweet caramelized onions in this recipe.

INGREDIENTS:

1 ½ tablespoons olive oil

½ large onion, diced or sliced thinly

2 teaspoons garlic powder

½ teaspoon Spike seasoning or salt and pepper

1-1 ½ pound kale (about 2 bunches), stems removed, washed, and torn

1 tablespoon balsamic vinegar

Makes: about 4 cups
Serving Size: ½ cup

1. Heat large pan over medium high heat. Add oil and onions and cook for two minutes, stirring frequently. Turn heat down to low. Cover and cook until onions are caramelized, approximately 30 minutes. Stir occasionally.

2. When onions are caramelized, add garlic, Spike, and kale. Cook until kale begins to wilt (about 3-5 minutes). Stir in balsamic vinegar and toss. Serve immediately.

Spaghetti Squash

Spaghetti squash is nature's pasta. It's a great gluten-free substitute for whole wheat pasta, and a colorful way to add fiber, calcium and vitamin A-rich squash to your menu.

INGREDIENTS:

1 spaghetti squash (about 2 pounds)

1 tablespoon unsalted butter

1 tablespoon chopped parsley

¾ teaspoon salt

¾ teaspoon of minced garlic

Makes: about 4 cups
Serving Size : ½ cup

1. Preheat oven to 375° F.

2. Carefully cut squash lengthwise. Scoop out seeds with a spoon. Be careful not to remove too much flesh. Place cut side down in a baking dish. Add ½ inch of water to the dish. Cover with aluminum foil and bake for 45 minutes.

3. When squash is easily pierced with a knife, turn over and bake for another 15 minutes. Remove from oven, uncover, and allow to cool enough to handle.

4. Using the tines of a fork, begin to scrape the flesh of the squash into a large bowl. Discard the skins. Add butter, parsley, salt, and garlic to the mixing bowl and toss to coat.

Entrée Recipes

 # BBQ Beef

This tangy, healthy rendition of a sloppy joe has less fat, less sugar and salt, and more fiber than the standard version thanks to the homemade sauce and the well-hidden veggies. When preparing for adults, spice it up with red pepper.

INGREDIENTS:

1 tablespoon olive or canola oil

½ cup Vidalia onion, small dice

¼ cup celery, fine dice

¼ cup carrots, fine dice

½ teaspoon garlic powder

½ teaspoon salt

1 cup tomato sauce

1 ½ pounds ground beef, raw (use minimum 90% lean ground beef)

2 tablespoons tomato paste

1 tablespoon brown sugar, unpacked

2 tablespoons apple cider vinegar

½ teaspoon dry mustard or 1 teaspoon prepared yellow mustard

1 tablespoon Worcestershire sauce

½ cup ketchup (corn-syrup-free)

¼ cup water, if needed

Makes: about 4 cups
Serving Size: ½ cup

1. Heat a large pan over medium high heat. Brown ground beef, remove from pan and drain fat.

2. Add oil, onions, celery, and carrots and sauté until onions are translucent and vegetables begin to soften. Add garlic and salt. Sauté another 3 minutes.

3. Add tomato sauce and combine well with vegetables. Cook until sauce begins to darken. Add remaining ingredients, including cooked beef. Bring to a boil and then reduce to a simmer. Simmer an additional 30 minutes. If thinner sauce is desired, add water to desired consistency. Serve on whole wheat bun.

Beef and Veggie Brown Rice Pilaf

Pilaf is a dish in which rice is cooked in a seasoned broth. In this healthy rendition, brown rice, lean beef, and low-sodium broth make a flavorful dish kids will love.

INGREDIENTS:

1 ½ pounds ground beef (use at least 90% lean)

1 tablespoon olive oil

½ medium onion, diced

1 stalk celery, chopped

¾ cup low sodium beef or vegetable stock

3 cups cooked brown rice

½ teaspoon Spike seasoning

½ teaspoon Lawry's seasoned salt

Pinch of black pepper

1 teaspoon dried parsley

½ teaspoon onion powder

Pinch of cayenne pepper

Makes: about 6 cups
Serving Size: 1 cup

1. In large skillet, sauté beef until browned. Drain fat.

2. Add olive oil, onion, and celery and sauté until soft, stirring occasionally.

3. Add broth and rice and bring to a simmer.

4. Add Spike, seasoned salt, pepper, parsley, onion powder, and cayenne.

5. Simmer on low for 15 minutes until rice is cooked through.

HOW TO COOK BROWN RICE:
Bring 1 cup of brown rice and 2 ½ cups of water to a boil in a medium sauce pan. Reduce heat to a low simmer, cover with a tight fitting lid, and cook until tender and the liquid has been absorbed. This should take about 40-50 minutes. Let stand for 5 minutes with the lid on, then fluff with a fork.
Yields 3 cups of cooked rice.

TIP: Consider serving this dish in a baked pepper for an extra dose of color.

Black Bean and Spinach Quesadilla

A quesadilla is like a Mexican-style stuffed pancake. It can be filled with any of your favorite vegetables, beans, meat, or cheese. It is a perfect lunch or snack food and is especially yummy when served with extra salsa or avocado dip.

INGREDIENTS:

½ tablespoon olive or canola oil

½ cup onion, small dice

1 ½ cups chopped frozen spinach (about 10 ounces), defrosted and squeezed dry

¼ teaspoon garlic powder

1 can (15 ounces) black beans, drained (Cuban black beans are especially wonderful in this recipe, see page 5)

6 whole wheat tortillas (8-10 inch)

3 cups reduced-fat cheddar cheese, shredded or reduced-fat Monterey jack cheese, shredded

1 ½ cups low sodium salsa

Olive oil mister or olive oil spray

Makes: 24 triangles
Serving size: 2-3 triangles

1. Preheat oven to 350° F. Heat large pan over medium high heat. Add oil and onions and sauté until onions are translucent. Add spinach and garlic and cook for 3 minutes to incorporate flavors. Keep warm.

2. Heat drained black beans and keep warm. For picky eaters, try mashing the black beans into a paste; add water if too dry.

3. When ready to fill tortillas, place the following on one half of a tortilla:

   ¼ cup spinach mixture
   ¼ cup beans
   ½ cup shredded cheese
   ¼ cup salsa

   Evenly spread the filling over the half to ½ inch from the edge. Fold tortilla over and press to seal. For a nice browned appearance, mist the top and bottom of each folded tortilla with olive oil.

4. Place quesadillas on parchment-lined or non-stick baking sheets. Bake until internal temperature reaches 165°F and cheese is melted, approximately 6-7 minutes. Remove from oven and let rest for a few minutes to let the cheese set. Cut each quesadilla into 4 triangles.

AVOCADO DIP goes especially well with quesadillas and is a great way to get in those healthy fats. Did you know that avocados have more potassium than bananas?

Purée the following ingredients in a food processor (or simply mash together in a bowl):

pulp from one avocado

$\frac{1}{3}$ cup plain Greek style non-fat yogurt

½ teaspoon Spike seasoning (or a pinch of salt and pepper)

Chicken and Cheese Quesadilla

This version of a quesadilla represents a typical Southwest United States preparation that involves ingredients sandwiched between two tortillas and then grilled or baked. Add sautéed vegetables to make this quesadilla extra delicious.

INGREDIENTS:

6 whole wheat tortillas (8-10 inch)

1 ½ cup shredded cheese, reduced-fat cheddar or reduced-fat Monterey jack cheese

½ pound cooked chicken, chopped

1 cup salsa (optional)

Makes: 12 triangles
Serving size: 1-2 triangles

1. Preheat oven to 350° F.

2. Place 3 tortillas on parchment-lined or non-stick baking sheets. Sprinkle each tortilla evenly with chicken and cheese. Place the remaining tortillas over the top.

3. Bake until internal temperature reaches 165° F and cheese is melted, approximately 6-7 minutes. Remove from oven and let rest for a few minutes to let cheese set. Cut each quesadilla into 4 triangles. Serve with salsa or avocado dip, if desired.

Creamy Butternut Squash Soup

Butternut squash is an excellent source of vitamins A and C, which increases the body's absorption of iron and aids in healing. This creamy and sweet soup is a fall and winter favorite.

INGREDIENTS:

1 average size butternut squash (2-3 pounds)

1 tablespoon butter

¾ cup onion, diced

1 carrot, peeled and diced

4 cups low-sodium vegetable or chicken broth

½ teaspoon salt

¼ teaspoon cinnamon

½ cup half and half

1 teaspoon brown sugar, unpacked

Makes: about 6 servings
Serving size: 1 cup

1. Preheat oven to 350° F. Quarter and seed butternut squash. Place cut side down in a baking dish. Add 1 inch of water to the dish. Cover with aluminum foil and bake for 60 minutes. Once cooled, drain and remove flesh from skin with spoon. Discard skins.

2. Heat butter in a large soup pot over medium heat. Add the onion and carrot and sauté until soft and fragrant, about 8 minutes. Be careful not to brown vegetables.

3. Add broth and butternut squash. Bring to a boil while stirring frequently. Lower heat to simmer. Add salt, cinnamon, and brown sugar. Remove from heat and allow to cool slightly.

4. Working in batches, carefully transfer the mixture to a blender/food processor (or use an immersion blender) and purée until very smooth. Return the purée to the pot and reheat over medium heat. Whisk in half and half. Adjust seasoning if desired.

Creamy Tomato Soup

Heating tomatoes helps to release many of their beneficial nutrients, especially cancer-fighting lycopene. Since lycopene is fat soluble, the half and half in this soup adds needed fat to help the body absorb even more of the tomatoes' potent antioxidants.

INGREDIENTS:

2 tablespoons olive oil or butter

¼ cup sweet onion (Vidalia), finely chopped

1 carrot, finely chopped

½ stalk celery, finely chopped

1 clove minced garlic

1 28-ounce can tomato pureé

4 cups low-sodium vegetable stock

2 tablespoons sugar

½ cup half and half

1 teaspoon Spike seasoning or salt

½ teaspoon black pepper

1. Heat the oil/butter in a large soup pot over medium heat. Add the onion, carrots, celery, and garlic and cook covered, stirring occasionally, until soft and fragrant, about 8 minutes.

2. Stir in the tomato pureé, vegetable broth, and sugar. Bring to a boil while whisking constantly. Lower the heat and simmer for 20 minutes. Remove from the heat and let cool slightly.

3. Working in batches, carefully transfer the mixture to a blender/food processor (or use an immersion blender) and pureé until very smooth. Return the pureé to the pot and reheat over medium heat.

4. Whisk in the half and half. Season with Spike or salt and pepper.

Makes: about 6 servings
Serving Size: 1 cup

Crustless Broccoli Quiche

Eggs are a great source of lean protein. This classic broccoli and cheese quiche dish (minus the crust) is a simple and flavorful way to enjoy the benefits of the versatile ingredient, eggs!

INGREDIENTS:

¼ cup onion, finely diced

1 tablespoon butter or olive oil

¾ cup low or non-fat cream cheese, softened

¾ cup milk, 1% or skim

6 large eggs

1 ½ teaspoons Spike seasoning

½ teaspoon garlic powder

3 cups frozen broccoli, chopped, thawed, and drained

2 cups reduced-fat sharp cheddar, shredded

Makes: 12 pieces
Serving Size: 1-2 pieces

1. In small sauté pan, cook onions in butter or olive oil until translucent. Set aside to cool.

2. In a mixer bowl, beat cream cheese until smooth. Add milk and beat until combined. Add eggs, Spike, and garlic. Fold in onions, broccoli, and cheese.

3. Coat a 9 x 11 inch pan with cooking spray, and then pour mixture into pan.

4. Bake in 350° F oven for about 35-40 minutes or until all liquid has set and top is golden brown. If the top starts to brown too quickly, cover lightly with aluminum foil. Cut each pan 3x4 inch servings.

"I could live off of this (quiche) and it even has broccoli in it!"
Beth Westmoreland, Director
A-B Tech Early
Education Center

Cuban Black Beans with Orange Zest

Fresh orange and lime juice provide a wonderful citrus tang that balances the earthy and savory flavor of black beans and cumin in this very popular black bean stew.

INGREDIENTS:

2 tablespoons olive oil

½ cup onion, small dice

2 cloves garlic, minced

½ teaspoon ground cumin

½ teaspoon dried oregano

5 cups black beans (about 3 15-ounce cans), drained and rinsed

2 cups vegetable stock or water

1 cup orange juice

2 tablespoons brown sugar

2 tablespoons lime juice

1 teaspoon orange zest

Makes: about 6 cups
Serving Size: 1 cup

1. In a large skillet, heat the oil over medium heat. Sauté the onion and garlic until they begin to soften. Add cumin and oregano and sauté for 1 minute, stirring often to prevent burning.

2. Add the black beans and vegetable stock or water, orange juice, and sugar if using. Simmer over medium heat until flavors blend, about 15-20 minutes. Stir often to prevent sticking.

3. Remove from heat. Mix in lime juice and orange zest. Serve with brown rice.

DID YOU KNOW that it can take 8-10 exposures to a new food before a child will eat it? Don't give up too soon!

Herb Roasted Turkey Breast

Turkey is low in fat and high in protein. It is a great alternative to chicken and is an inexpensive source of Vitamin B, potassium, iron, and zinc.

INGREDIENTS:

1 tablespoon olive oil

1 teaspoon dried sage

1 teaspoon dried rosemary

1 teaspoon dried thyme

½ teaspoon garlic powder

½ teaspoon Spike seasoning or salt and pepper

2 pounds boneless, skinless turkey breast

Makes: about 6 servings
Serving Size: 3-4 ounces

1. In large zip top bag, mix olive oil, sage, rosemary, thyme, garlic, and Spike. Shake to combine.

2. Between sheets of parchment paper or plastic wrap, gently pound out the thickest part of the turkey breast with a mallet or heavy rolling pin to create a uniform thickness.

3. Add the turkey to the bag with the marinade and gently shake the bag to coat evenly. Marinate in the refrigerator for a minimum of 1 hour (best if left overnight).

4. Place turkey in baking pan and pour marinade on top. Bake at 375° F for 1 to 1½ hours, until the thickest part of turkey breast reaches 160° F. Remove from oven, cover with foil, and allow to rest for 5-10 minutes before serving.

Lemon Herb Chicken Breast

The lemon and herb marinade adds a wonderful citrus flavor, while the olive oil helps keep the skinless breast moist and tender during cooking.

INGREDIENTS:

2 tablespoons olive oil

2 teaspoons lemon juice

½ teaspoon Spike or salt and pepper

½ teaspoon dried thyme

1 ½ pounds chicken breast, boneless, skinless

Makes: 6 servings
Serving size: 3-4 ounces

1. Put the olive oil, lemon juice, Spike, and herbs in a large zip top bag. Close the bag and shake to combine all the ingredients.

2. Between sheets of parchment paper, pound out the thickest part of the chicken breast with a mallet or heavy rolling pin. Drop the chicken breast in the bag with the marinade and shake the bag to coat evenly. Marinate for a minimum of 1 hour (best if left overnight).

3. Place in baking dish and bake for approximately 25 minutes at 375° F or until the thickest part of chicken breast reaches 160° F. Remove from oven, cover with foil, and allow to rest for 5-10 minutes before serving. NOTE: cooking times vary based on thickness of chicken.

This chicken also works well on the grill or sautéed in a pan with a small amount of olive oil.

Mac and Cheese

Everyone goes mad for this classic comfort food. It is such a popular food that it stays on our menu year-round. No one will know that it is made with reduced-fat cheddar and has half the salt and fat of a conventional cheese sauce.

INGREDIENTS:

8 ounces whole wheat elbow macaroni noodles

¼ cup unsalted butter

¼ cup all-purpose flour

½ teaspoon mustard, dry

¾ teaspoon salt

2 cups milk, 1% or skim

2 ½ cups reduced-fat cheddar cheese, shredded

¼ cup parmesan cheese, shredded

½ cup whole wheat bread crumbs

1. Preheat oven to 350° F. In large pot, bring water to a boil and cook pasta. Drain and set aside.

2. In large saucepan (or skillet), melt butter and then add flour and dry mustard to make a roux. Stir until incorporated, about 3 minutes. Do not brown.

3. In saucepan or in the microwave, heat milk until it is warm. Slowly add heated milk to flour mixture, whisking continuously. Cook until smooth and thickened (10-15 minutes) or until the raw flour taste is cooked out.

4. Whisk the cheeses into the sauce a little at a time to prevent clumping. Stir over low heat until cheese is fully melted.

5. Combine macaroni and sauce and mix well. Place mac and cheese mixture into a deep 8" by 8" pan which has been lightly coated with pan release spray. Bake for 30 minutes, then sprinkle with bread crumbs and bake for another 10 minutes or until top becomes golden brown and internal temperature reaches 165° F.

Makes: about 8 servings
Serving size: ¾-1 cup

Oven Baked Chicken Strips

These little strips are fast to prepare and delicious to eat. They are low in sodium and have less fat than the fried alternatives. Eat plain or with your favorite dipping sauce. To make a gluten-free version, use crushed corn flakes cereal instead of bread crumbs.

INGREDIENTS:

1 ½ pounds boneless, skinless chicken breast

1 large egg

½ cup low-fat buttermilk

1 cup whole wheat bread crumbs

½ teaspoon Spike seasoning or salt and pepper

½ teaspoon dried thyme

Makes: about 18 pieces
Serving Size: 3 pieces

1. Preheat oven to 400° F degrees. Cut chicken breasts into strips (about 1 ounce each). In large bowl, mix eggs and buttermilk. Add chicken. Cover and refrigerate for 30 minutes.

2. In medium bowl, mix bread crumbs, and Spike, and thyme. Set aside. Roll strips in bread crumbs to coat.

3. Line a baking sheet with parchment. You can also use a non-stick baking sheet. Place breaded chicken on pan. Bake for about 20 minutes or until internal temperature has reached 165° F.

Pasta with Beef Bolognese

This version of spaghetti and meat sauce features a protein-rich whole wheat pasta that contains healthy amounts of fiber and antioxidants. Pasta sauce is a great place to hide vegetables for picky eaters.

INGREDIENTS:

8 ounces whole wheat penne pasta

1 ½ pounds lean ground beef

½ cup onion, chopped

3 cups vegetable marinara sauce

½ cup part-skim shredded mozzarella cheese

Makes: about 6 cups
Serving size: 1 cup

> **PREPARATION NOTE:**
>
> Pasta and sauce may be made the day before and refrigerated. Portion into a baking pan, cover with parchment and foil (tightly wrapped) and reheat at 350°F to an internal temperature of 165° F.

PURCHASE NOTES:
If you are using prepared marinara sauce, choose one that does not contain high fructose corn syrup and has less than 350 mg sodium per ½ cup serving.

1. Heat water to a rolling boil. Slowly add pasta while stirring constantly until water boils again. Cook according to package directions. Do not overcook. Drain well.

2. Brown ground beef. Add onions to ground beef and sauté for 5 minutes or until onions are translucent. Drain all oil from beef mixture.

3. In heavy pot, combine beef and onion mixture with marinara sauce. Bring to boil over medium heat. Reduce heat, cover, and simmer for 10 minutes, stirring occasionally.

4. Stir pasta into meat sauce and heat to a minimum of 165° F.

5. Top each portion with 1 tablespoon of mozzarella cheese.

Red Lentil Stew with Coconut Curry

The soup is fashioned after dahl, a thick lentil soup traditionally served in India. This colorful, full bodied stew is seasoned with mild curry and sweet, creamy coconut milk and is the perfect dish for a cold day.

INGREDIENTS:

12 ounces dried red lentils (or yellow split peas)

2 ¼ cup water

1 tablespoon extra virgin olive oil

¼ cup onion, finely chopped

2-3 teaspoons mild curry powder

1 teaspoon salt

7 ounces low-fat coconut milk

2 teaspoons lemon juice

1 tablespoon unsalted butter

Makes: about 6 cups
Serving Size: 1 cup

Purchase Note:
If you can't find red lentils, chickpeas are a great substitute. Use 2 15-ounce cans (roughly 3 cups drained) for this recipe. Mash slightly to thicken consistency.

1. Give the lentils a good rinse until the water poured off is no longer murky. Place them in a large soup pot, cover with water, and bring to a boil. Reduce heat and simmer for about 20-30 minutes until lentils are soft.

2. While lentils are cooking, heat olive oil in small skillet over medium heat and add onion. Sauté until soft. If onions start to brown, reduce the heat. Cook for 10 minutes. Add curry powder and cook for 2 minutes. Add to lentils and continue cooking until lentils are soft.

3. Remove from heat and add salt, coconut milk, lemon juice, and butter, purée with an immersion blender or in a food processor until smooth. Reheat until lightly boiling. Adjust consistency with warm water, if needed.

Serve over brown rice or quinoa.

Spinach and Feta Frittata

Veggie frittatas are a crustless quiche that can feature an ever-changing selection of seasonal vegetables.

INGREDIENTS:

¼ cup onion, finely diced

1 tablespoon olive oil

1 cup frozen spinach, thawed and squeezed dry

4 large eggs

½ cup 1% or skim milk

½ cup non-fat sour cream

¼ tablespoon Spike seasoning or salt and pepper

¼ teaspoon garlic powder

¼ cup reduced-fat sharp cheddar cheese, shredded

⅓ cup reduced-fat feta cheese, crumbled

Makes: about 6 pieces
Serving Size: 1 piece

1. Preheat oven to 350° F. Lightly oil a 9-inch pie pan.

2. In small sauté pan, cook onions in oil until translucent. Add spinach and cook for 5 minutes. Allow mixture to cool.

3. In large bowl, add egg, milk, sour cream, and seasonings. Whisk until combined. Fold in spinach/ onion mixture and cheese.

4. Pour the mixture into the pan.

5. Bake for 35-45 minutes or until all liquid has set and the top is golden brown. If the top starts to brown too quickly, cover lightly with aluminum foil.

Spinach Lasagna

This lower-fat lasagna is rich and delicious. It will be your little secret that it is made with reduced-fat cheese and has half the salt and fat of traditional lasagna. This recipe is a favorite for all ages.

INGREDIENTS:

9 lasagna noodles

½ cup frozen spinach, thawed, drained

4 ounces ricotta cheese, part skim

16 ounces low-fat or 1% cottage cheese

⅓ cup parmesan cheese

½ teaspoon salt

½ teaspoon dried oregano

½ teaspoon dried basil

¼ teaspoon granulated garlic

¼ teaspoon Spike seasoning or salt and pepper

1 large egg, beaten

2 ½ cups marinara sauce

1 ¼ cups part-skim mozzarella cheese, grated

Makes: about 6 servings
Serving Size: 1 piece

1. Preheat oven to 350° F. In large pot, bring water to boil and cook lasagna noodles 8-11 minutes or until al dente.

2. Squeeze out all excess liquid from spinach until nearly dry. Combine ricotta cheese, cottage cheese, Parmesan cheese, spinach, salt, oregano, basil, garlic, Spike, and egg in bowl. Mix thoroughly. Separate cheese mixture evenly into two small bowls.

3. Spray one 11"x7" pan with pan release spray. Spread bottom of pan with ½ cup pasta sauce.

ASSEMBLY:

First Layer:
3 lasagna noodles
Contents of one small bowl of cheese mixture
½ cup mozzarella
1 cup marinara sauce

Second layer:
3 lasagna noodles
1 cup marinara sauce
½ cup mozzarella

Top with three remaining noodles, ½ cup marinara sauce, and ¼ cup mozzarella cheese.

4. Bake covered for 30 minutes. TIP: If you spray your aluminum foil or your cover with pan spray, the cheese won't stick.

5. Remove cover and put back in oven for additional 30 minutes or until heated through to 165°F or higher. Remove from oven and allow to sit for 15 minutes before serving. Cut pan 2x3 (6 pieces).

WHAT'S COOKING? Children love to help in the kitchen and cooking teaches problem solving, math, measuring, science, and language. It even supports motor development, creativity, and introduces children to other cultures. Even preschoolers are very capable of helping in the kitchen (always with constant supervision). They can wash and tear lettuce greens, break things into pieces (bread or green beans, for example), dip, stir, and add ingredients. As they get a little older, they can pour, spread, use a cookie cutter, assemble a pizza, count ingredients, and knead dough, shake, and mix. As children gain experience, they can cut soft fruit with a plastic knife, peel some foods, toss a salad, set the table, and help make sandwiches.

Spinach Pesto Pasta

This dish is made with fresh spinach and sunflower seeds for a healthy, protein-packed pasta. Have extra on hand because children can't get enough of this iron-rich, cheesy pasta.

INGREDIENTS:

2 cups fresh baby spinach, packed

¼ cup roasted sunflower seeds

½ cup Parmesan cheese, grated

1 garlic clove, minced

½ teaspoon lemon juice

¼ cup olive oil

8 ounces whole wheat or fiber enriched pasta

Makes: about 6 servings
Serving Size: 1 cup

1. Place all ingredients except pasta and oil in food processor. Pulse to combine. With food processor running, drizzle in olive oil. Adjust consistency with warm water, if necessary.

2. In large pot, cook pasta until just done. When ready, drain and set aside in large bowl. Spoon in pesto and mix with warm pasta to coat.

This pasta is served hot, but makes a great cold salad when mixed with a little bit of low-fat mayonnaise.

Studies show that eating together as a family increases consumption of healthy foods, increases vocabulary, raises self-esteem, increases grade point averages, and fosters family relationships. Make it a goal to sit down as a family for 3-5 meals each week.

Squash Casserole

Squash casserole is a Southern favorite. This healthy version has all of the flavor of traditional squash casserole with less fat and more protein.

INGREDIENTS

6 cups summer squash (about 3-4 medium), quartered and sliced

½ onion, small dice

3 large eggs

1 cup non-fat sour cream

½ cup skim milk

1 teaspoon salt

¼ teaspoon granulated garlic (or fresh garlic clove, minced)

2-2 ½ cups reduced-fat cheddar cheese, shredded

Makes: about 6 servings
Serving Size: 1 cup

1. Preheat oven to 350° F. Put squash and onion in pot with about a ½ inch of water. Cover tightly and steam for 5-7 minutes or until tender. Drain vegetables well and cool slightly.

2. In separate bowl, beat eggs. Add sour cream, milk, salt, garlic, and ½ of the cheese.

3. Put vegetables in an 8" x 8" casserole dish (or a similar size). Gently fold in the egg mixture. Top with remaining cheese. Bake for 35-40 minutes or until liquid has set and the top is bubbly. Allow to rest for 10 minutes.

CREATE HEALTHIER CELEBRATIONS by including some non-food fun. Here are some suggestions for celebrating without lots of added salt and sugar!

- Give age-appropriate goodies such as stickers, pencils, erasers, or bookmarks
- Use fun plates, napkins, and cups for healthy snacks
- Make a sash, crown, or badge to celebrate a birthday child
- Have a parade or dance party
- Go on a picnic!
- Let your child choose a favorite activity for that day.
- Decorate!

Sweet and Sour Chicken

Enjoy the Asian favorite with a side of brown rice. Add pineapple chunks or your favorite stir-fried vegetables for adventurous variations. You can even try this tangy sauce with other proteins.

INGREDIENTS:

3 tablespoons olive oil

1 ½ pounds skinless chicken breast cut into 1" cubes

¼ cup corn starch

¼ cup cold water

1 cup unsweetened pineapple juice

3 tablespoons brown sugar, unpacked

¼ cup white vinegar

3 tablespoons low-sodium soy sauce

1 teaspoon garlic powder

1 tablespoon tomato paste

Makes: about 5-6 servings
Serving Size: 3-4 ounce

1. In large skillet, heat oil over medium heat. Add chicken and cook through.

2. In small bowl or cup, whisk together cornstarch and cold water to create a paste. Set aside.

3. In saucepan, add all other ingredients. Bring to a boil and then simmer for 5 minutes. Add corn starch mixture and simmer for another 3 minutes. Remove from heat and allow to cool and thicken for another 3 minutes. Pour over chicken or serve sauce on the side.

Tangy Meatloaf

This tangy ketchup-infused meatloaf is perfect on a slice of warm bread. Serve with ketchup or barbecue sauce. When serving to adults, spice up the ketchup with cayenne.

INGREDIENTS:

1 teaspoon olive or canola oil

1 tablespoon Vidalia onion, finely chopped

1 pound lean ground beef

1 tablespoon whole wheat bread crumbs

1 egg, beaten

1 teaspoon Spike seasoning (or salt and pepper)

½ teaspoon garlic powder

⅓ cup ketchup

2 teaspoons Worcestershire sauce

Combine the following ingredients to make the glaze:

⅓ cup ketchup

3 tablespoons barbecue sauce

1 teaspoon Worcestershire sauce

Makes: about 6 servings
Serving Size: 1 slice

1. Preheat oven to 350° F.

2. Heat large pan over medium high heat. Add oil and sauté onion until translucent and lightly caramelized.

3. In large bowl, combine onions, ground beef, bread crumbs, egg, spike, and garlic powder. Mix ketchup and Worcestershire sauce together in small bowl and add to meat mixture; mix well.

4. Shape mixture into loaf pan. Bake for 30 minutes. Carefully drain off any fat that has collected in the pan and spread the glaze mixture evenly on top. Bake until internal temperature is 165° F and meat loaf is cooked through, approximately 1 hour.

LOOK for ketchup and BBQ sauce that does not contain high fructose corn syrup.

Turkey Meatballs

These versatile meatballs may be served plain or smothered in a variety of sauces. They are enhanced with sunflower seeds and vegetables, but their delicious taste will never give away their nutritional value!

INGREDIENTS:

2 teaspoons olive or canola oil

½ cup onion, small dice

½ cup mushrooms, small dice

1 ¼ pounds lean ground turkey

1 large egg

3 tablespoons sunflower seeds, salted and roasted

¼ cup whole wheat bread crumbs

¼ teaspoon Spike seasoning or salt and pepper

⅛ teaspoon garlic powder

Makes: about 18 meatballs
Serving Size: 3 meatballs

1. Preheat oven to 400° F.

2. Heat large pan over medium-high heat. Add oil, onions, and mushrooms and sauté until onions are translucent and mushrooms begin to soften. Let cool.

3. In large bowl, combine the turkey and onion mixture with the rest of the ingredients. Mix well.

4. Line baking pan with parchment paper (or use a non-stick baking pan). Using a tablespoon, scoop about 1½ ounces of mixture and form into balls. Place on baking sheet. Bake for 15-20 minutes until browned and cooked through, and the internal temperature has reached 165° F.

White Bean and Spinach Stew

This Rainbow In My Tummy® favorite is a quick and simple stew with fairly flexible ingredients. For variety, feel free to use your favorite greens, herbs, and spices. Protein-packed hearty cannellini beans are not only tasty, but very nutritious with twice the iron of beef.

INGREDIENTS:

¼ cup vegetable oil

1 cup celery, diced

1 cup onion, diced

1 teaspoon granulated garlic

¼ teaspoon thyme

2 cups lightly packed baby spinach, chopped

2 cups vegetable or chicken broth

3 cups (2 15-ounce cans) cannellini beans, rinsed and drained

¼ teaspoon Spike seasoning (or salt and pepper)

2-3 teaspoons lemon juice

Makes: about 6 cups
Serving Size: 1 cup

PURCHASE NOTES:
Great Northern beans are a great substitute for cannellini beans.

1. Heat oil in large soup pot over medium low heat. Add celery and onion and cook for about 7 minutes, until soft. Add garlic and thyme and cook for 1 minute. Add chopped spinach and cook for 2 minutes.

2. Add broth, beans, and seasoning. Reduce heat to medium-low and simmer for 5 minutes.

3. Mix in lemon juice. Add additional broth to adjust consistency, if desired. Cover and cook over medium heat for 10 minutes.

Yukon Gold Potato Leek Soup

Leeks offer a milder, sweeter flavor than onions. In this recipe, they are perfectly paired with vitamin C-packed potatoes and calcium-rich dairy to make this delicious cool weather classic a hearty and nutritious soup.

INGREDIENTS:

3 tablespoons unsalted butter

1 leek (white and light green part only), washed well, sliced thinly, then chopped

1 ½ pounds Yukon gold potatoes, peeled and cubed

5 cups chicken or vegetable broth

¼ tablespoon fresh thyme, finely chopped, or 1 teaspoon dried thyme

½ teaspoon salt

⅛ teaspoon black pepper

¾ cup half and half

Makes: about 6 cups
Serving size: 1 cup

1. Heat butter in large pot over medium low heat. Add leeks and cook for about 10 minutes, until tender. Be careful not to brown or burn leeks.

2. Add potatoes, broth, and thyme. Bring to a boil, then simmer for 25-30 minutes, until potatoes are tender. Add salt and pepper.

3. Using immersion blender or blender, blend soup to desired consistency. Add half and half.

Healthy Snacks

Choose one item from two of the food groups listed below. Serve the same types of food you would at breakfast, lunch or dinner. Try to structure snack times so that they happen at about the same time each day and are eaten at the table (as often as possible). This prevents constant grazing and helps children eat more regularly at meal time. These are just a few suggestions and some are a natural fit: fruit with yogurt, hummus on pita, and nut butter on celery. By all means, be creative! You and your child may find some new favorite snack pairs!

Fruit	Vegetable	Protein/Dairy	Grain
Banana	Vegetable sticks (carrot, celery, cucumber, zucchini, etc.)	Hummus (try our Sweet Potato Hummus)	Whole grain crackers
Apple slices			Toast
Kiwi	Edamame	Part skim cheeses	Whole wheat pita
Orange slices	Cherry tomatoes (sliced)	Nut butters	Baked tortilla triangles (not fried)
Mango slices	Broccoli stalks	Unsweetened or lightly sweetened yogurt	Whole grain English muffin
Strawberries	Pepper slices (green, red, yellow, or orange)	Bean dips	Whole grain pretzels
Berries		Hard-boiled egg	Whole wheat mini bagel
Watermelon	Sugar snap peas	Scrambled egg	Whole grain cereal (low sugar)
Grapes (sliced)	Cauliflower pieces	Low-fat cream cheese	Instant oatmeal
Dried fruit (chopped for younger children)	String beans	Slices or cubes of lean meat	Plain popcorn (for older children)
Pear slices	Avocados	Skim milk	Whole wheat pasta
Sliced apricots		Part skim cottage cheese	Bagel chips
Melon slices		Chicken or tuna salad	Whole grain tortilla
Pineapple chunks			Whole grain waffle
Plums			

Vegetable — Note: Be sure to chop into small pieces and lightly steam to soften for younger eaters.
Serving size: about ½ cup

Protein/Dairy — **Serving size: ½ ounce** or 2 tablespoons of spreads such as hummus

Grain — **Serving size: ¼ -⅓ cup** or about ½ slice of bread

Fruit — Note: Be sure to chop into small pieces for younger eaters.
Serving size: about ½ cup (¼ cup if dried fruit)

Top Tips for Introducing New Foods

🍎 Patience is a virtue. Offer new foods many times and don't get upset if your child doesn't eat them at first.

🍎 Let your child pick out a new food at the grocery store.

🍎 Introduce new foods one at a time and serve them alongside familiar favorties.

🍎 Involve children in preparing food. They can stir, pour, and set the table, for example.

🍎 Set a good example by trying (and liking!) new foods yourself.

🍎 Let your child try small portions at first.

🍎 Eat together as a family. Eating in a relaxed setting can increase willingess to try new things.

🍎 Don't use food as a reward or punishment.

🍎 Avoid a power struggle. Don't get upset if your child doesn't take to a new food right away.

🍎 Have fun! Trying new foods is fun!

Preparation and Shopping Guide

The Rainbow In My Tummy® program has been able to improve the quality of food served to young children by making straightforward changes and holding fast to some basic principles when shopping. In general, RIMT menus simply use more fresh fruits and vegetables, more whole grains, less saturated fat, and less added sugar and salt. Here are some shopping tips to make shopping for Rainbow In My Tummy® menus uncomplicated and trouble-free.

Fresh fruits and vegetables: Purchase fresh fruits and vegetables from the produce section of the grocery store. Look for items that are in season. If you cannot find what you are looking for fresh, the next best option is frozen. Frozen produce is flash frozen at peak ripeness, which maintains the nutrients at their highest quality and availability. Try to stay away from canned fruits and vegetables as much as you can. If you do purchase canned products, choose food packed in its own juice or water. Always rinse canned items before serving; this will help decrease added sugar and salt.

Whole grains: This simply refers to grains that are not processed or refined. Choose brown rice over white rice, whole grain breads and pastas instead of white breads and pastas. Look for packages that say "100% whole wheat," for example, not just "whole grain." If you see the words "enriched" or "de-germinated" in the ingredient list, leave the item on the shelf. Choose items that list a whole grain first, such as "whole wheat flour" or "whole oats."

Saturated fat: Meat and dairy products are the two biggest sources of saturated fat in the American diet. So, how do you get less of it in a diet? Select low-fat or non-fat dairy products when you buy milk, cheese, and yogurt. Children do not need whole milk after the age of 2. When buying meat, choose extra-lean when using ground, and trim the visible fat off cuts of meat before cooking. Unsaturated fat is a fat that comes from plants and this is the type that you want to have in your diet. Nuts, vegetable oils, and fish are all foods that have unsaturated fat.

Added sugar and salt: Sugar and salt both occur in foods naturally, but they are also added to processed foods to help make them tastier and last longer on the shelf. These "added" ingredients are the ones to have less of in our diets. To reduce these ingredients, stay away from ready-to-eat and processed foods. Look for cereals that have 6 grams or less of sugar per serving, and try to keep salt to a maximum of 600mg per meal.

PHOTO CREDITS

The Rainbow In My Tummy® Family Cookbook
was made possible by:

AN INITIATIVE OF THE
KATE B. REYNOLDS CHARITABLE TRUST